RED Robin

Boost Mobile
3099660919

The Illuminati

The history and truth behind the Illuminati

6302105751
LeLe Mom

Chivalry -

Table Of Contents

Introduction

I want to thank you and congratulate you for downloading the book, "*The Illuminati: The History and Truth Behind The Illuminati.*"

This book contains helpful information about the Illuminati, the history behind it, and common beliefs about it.

Through reading this book, you will discover how the Illuminati was founded, its original members, and the primary goals of the organization when it was first conceptualized.

As time passed, the Illuminati was supposedly shut down and ceased to exist. However, many conspiracy theorists believe that the Illuminati continued to live on, with some particularly sinister motives.

You will soon discover many of the conspiracy theories regarding the Illuminati, and how the Illuminati may in fact be still running the show. This includes their influence in the entertainment industry, political world, and their plans for the future of the world as a whole!

This book will provide you with all you need to know about the Illuminati, including the truth behind it, and the common beliefs and misconceptions regarding it!

Thanks again for downloading this book, I hope you enjoy it!

Chapter 1:
The Early Beginnings Of The Illuminati

There are many different things that have been said about the Illuminati; there plenty of misconceptions and theories that have also contributed to their infamy in more modern times. They have been referred to as one of the most powerful secret societies in the world; the ones pulling the strings and implementing major events that significantly affect mankind, all done in a bid for world domination. But is this the truth? Are the Illuminati really the villainous masked men that they are often portrayed to be?

Let's begin with the original Illuminati order.

According to existing documents, the Bavarian Illuminati (also known as the Ancient Illuminated Seers of Bavaria) was founded by Adam Weishaupt, a professor of Practical Philosophy and Canon Law at the University of Ingolstadt on May 1st 1776. Some years prior to his appointment at the university, the suppression of the Society of Jesus (the Jesuits) was put into action by Pope Clement XIV. This led to Jesuits losing the positions they held in the universities that they founded themselves. In fact, in his youth, Weishaupt was educated by the same group.

When Weishaupt was given the university position, it was considered to be quite controversial by people who were both hostile and friendly towards the Jesuits. As for his time there, there are also conflicting reports about this. Some say that he was quite hostile towards the Jesuits as well as the Catholic Church. However, there are also reports that talk of his own bad experiences from the ex-Jesuits that did remain in the university and were not keen on the more liberal courses being taught at the time. Many speak of the latter as being the catalyst, the reason as to why Weishaupt founded the Illuminati.

It was the Bavarian order's goal to free the people's minds from both superstition and prejudice. They encouraged people to be good, and taught them that this is the path to happiness. Keep in mind that Bavaria, at this time, was intensely Catholic and people's fear of superstition was certainly prevalent. They were heavily against the influence of religion in the people's daily lives and opposed abuses of state power. Many people shared the same ideals, yet membership grew rather slowly for the order.

When it was first formed, there were only five members within it. Weishaupt and four law students: Massenhausen, Merz, Bauhof and Sutor. All five took to using aliases during their meetings and were respectively known within the order as *Spartacus, Ajax, Tiberius, Agathon and Erasmus Roterodamus*. Sutor was expelled from the order due to indolence.

Massenhausen spearheaded the recruitment and expansion of the group, bringing in Xavier von Zwack who was one of Weishaupt's former students. A series of events followed this and in the end, Masshenhausen cut ties with the order. At this time, Zwack had control of the order's Munich group and the total membership had risen to twelve. The climb for the order in terms of membership remained slow despite Zwack's efforts. It was in 1780, when Baron Adolphe Francois Frederic Knigge (alias: Philo) joined the group. Along with him came the rituals which were used for 3 degrees of symbolic Freemasonry, along with ten more that were being used within the Illuminati. From 1780 to 1783, the membership for the Illuminati grew from a dozen to over 3,000.

Bavaria

In great numbers comes strength, one that the government did not overlook. By late 1783, there were rumors circulating that the Illuminati order intended to change the government and impose their own ideals on the land. Fearing the end of his reign, Duke Karl Theodor, the Elector Palatinate of Bavaria at the time, began to issue Edicts which ordered the suppression of the Illuminati. The first was sent out on June 22, 1784 and was repeated twice more in 1785. Once these Edicts were out, being associated with the Illuminati became unsafe for members who were in Bavaria.

There were consequences for its founder too, of course. In 1785, Weishaupt was removed from his University post and subsequently banished from Bavaria. He was offered a pension but refused it. Duke Ernst II of SachsenGothaAlternburg, Thuringia, Germany provided him with asylum and a University of Gottingen post. This is where he spent the rest of his years as a professor up until he died on November 18, 1830.

The Later Years:

Information about the order's goals and rituals was actually collected from the writings published by Weishaupt from 1785 onwards. Others were obtained from the search of all the letters and papers which were found in the residence of Xavier von Zwack. This search was able to acquire at least 200 different letters, including exchanges between Weishaupt as well as the other leaders of the Illuminati. There is some debate about the Zwack documents, saying that they were not meant for the public, but that the intended audience was the state itself. It was during the late 1700's that the government became quite hostile towards secret societies, after all. They were undoubtedly threatened, especially by ones that had powerful and rich men as members- the Illuminati among those.

It would come as no surprise to anyone that after the 1784 Edicts, the members in the Bavarian Illuminati rapidly declined. However, they left a number of literature and inspired an even greater number of books to be written about them. Authors who were hostile towards the Illuminati as well as Masonry first put out their "review" of the secret societies, many of which were rather harsh and contained inaccuracies. Even the masons put out literature condemning the Bavarian Illuminati, stating that the order deserved no more than a footnote when it comes to history.

However, this was not to be the case.

Chapter 2: Modern Conspiracy Theories About The Illuminati

Though history tells us that the Illuminati was dissolved by 1875, there are modern conspiracy theorists who believe that this is not entirely factual. In fact, many of them say that the Illuminati was never really disbanded. The group simply went deeper underground where they kept on recruiting members and spreading their philosophies. Seems harmless enough, right? Not quite.

There is a darker version to this story and it begins with Weishaupt's move to Germany. History tells us that he spent the rest of his life as a university professor and that when he died, what was left of the order died along with him. Conspiracy theorists will disagree, of course, for it is their belief that Weishaupt never ceased his correspondence with members of the order. All that time, he was merely putting up a facade whilst continuously spreading enlightenment and expanding the philosophy of a one world government.

The Rebirth:

What this theory suggests is that the freethinking order, the same people who sought freedom from abuse of power, have since changed their motives and are now pushing for world domination. Sounds a little farfetched, right? These conspiracy theorists say otherwise and that if the average man simply took more time to understand and really look at what's happening around them, they would find that the evidence is right out in the open.

Today, the Illuminati is more commonly perceived as a secret cabal that's comprised of some of the world's most powerful and rich men. From the shadows, they are supposedly controlling many people in positions of power as well as global economic leaders. They infiltrate multinational corporations as well as governments, making their way to the highest ranks while gaining political power and influence. All of this is done in preparation for the New World order.

Influence on Society and History:

Ever since the founding and supposed dissolution of the Bavarian Illuminati order, many theories have been put forward which blame the order for many significant events which put big changes into action. For example, there is a great number of people who believe that the Illuminati was behind the French Revolution. It was their enlightened propaganda that ignited the spark and fanned the flames of the revolution itself. But it doesn't end there.

Aside from the French Revolution, many other historical events are said to have been orchestrated by the Illuminati. Among them:

- The American Revolution
- The Assassination of President Kennedy
- Waterloo
- World War I
- World War II
- The Rise of Communism

Every event is said to have been put into play as a bid to weaken world powers and hasten the success of their domination. For example, according to some conspiracy theorists, World War I was orchestrated as a means of destroying Czarism in Russia and eventually, to establish the country as a stronghold for Communism. Every step is calculated and because the rest of the world is unaware, they are able forward their plans with relative ease.

The same also applies to World War II which saw the Fascists being pitted against so-called political Zionists in order to build up Communism to a point where it equaled the united strength of Christendom. *In the future?* A World War III is supposedly in the Illuminati masterplan and this is meant to pit Muslim or Islamic ruled nations against Western nations. Should this succeed, the war would affect the global economy and bring it to its knees. At this time, the different nations of the world would have no choice but to submit to the One World Government system and be controlled by the Illuminati.

A scary thought isn't it? Even scarier is the fact that these conspiracy theorists believe that the Illuminati influence is everywhere and that the New World Order plan is already moving forward. In fact, some even say that we're already seeing the beginning stages of it and if nothing is being done to stop it? We might be experiencing this New World Order much sooner than we think. When we do realize it, it may all be too late.

Chapter 3:
Illuminati's Supposed Influence On Popular Culture

When we speak of popular culture, the first things that come to mind are books, movies and music - seemingly innocent sources of entertainment that we indulge ourselves in regularly. However, would you still be able to look at them in the same way once you've learned that these things might actually be connected to the Illuminati? In this context, we speak of the secret cabal that's supposedly hell bent on world domination; the group of people that conspiracy theorists believe to be running things from behind the shadows.

Let's begin with movies that are said to be part of the Illuminati propaganda.

Many conspiracy theorists believe that the influence of the order on Hollywood all started with the Stanley Kubrick film, Eyes Wide Shut. It was one of the first to publicize and utilize the idea that there are secret societies that exist. Part of the controversy surrounding the Illuminati association of this film would be the director's death just months before the movie's release. It has been suggested that Kubrick's commitment to getting the movie out there, and in some way informing the public about secret societies in existence, was what led to his mysterious and untimely death.

The portrayal of the secret cabal in the film became deeply associated with the Illuminati itself - robes, masks, mysterious rituals and exclusive meetings that required passwords. These things became the “popular” image for what being in the real Illuminati is like.

Another movie that tackles the idea of a secret cabal would be Dan Brown's Angels and Demons. The book itself was turned into a popular movie in 2009 and exposed the idea to a far greater audience than what Eyes Wide Shut was able to access. In this thriller, the protagonist races against time in an effort to stop a secret religious society, the Illuminati, from its bid to destroy the entirety of the Vatican City. In the movie, they portray both sides as having secrets of their own and the protagonist has to learn about some of these secrets in order to succeed. In the end, the Vatican concedes to letting him access the Vatican's basements where the secret archives are kept; all of it, protected by bullet proof glass.

The reality? The archive exists, but within a wing. Some call it a fortress, located behind St. Peter's Basilica. This building is protected by an entire phalanx of Swiss Guards as well as officers from the state's Gendarmerie. Contained within its walls are 52 miles of shelving as well as antique wooden cabinets, all of which hold the church's priceless collections of different parchment letters that were sent by potentates, princes and heretics to the Holy See. It also includes correspondence between the Vatican and some of the most prominent figures throughout history such as Charlemagne, Erasmus, Mozart, Michelangelo, Voltaire, Queen Elizabeth I, and Adolf Hitler.

So the idea of secrets being kept hidden behind those walls isn't too farfetched and makes the idea more believable for the viewer. In fact, many people have taken the contents of this book to be real, or at least as clues as to what's being hidden from them.

Now, take these two films and look at them more closely. Eyes Wide Shut portrays the secret order as the villain of its plot. On the other hand, Angels and Demons portrays them as a group that seeks to enlighten and destroy the hand (the Vatican) that's been keeping all the secrets from the people. A surprising shift, right? Conspiracy theorists say it is all part of the propaganda. Instead of scaring people with all the secrecy and exclusivity, they're opening themselves up to the greater public but with utmost control over what is revealed.

"If they need to know who we are, we'll be the ones dictating what they can and can't know."

Through popular culture mediums such as books, movies and films, they are able to give a distorted picture of what the order really is about. A more romantic, less sinister look at what their intentions are and the means they take in order to achieve their goals. The approach is clearly successful, of course. There are a lot of people who are fascinated by the idea; some are even volunteering to join. The order has become quite mythical in a sense, exuding a sense of adventure and truthfulness that conspiracy theorists say are all mere facades.

Shortlist of movies that feature the Illuminati and similar ideals:

- Equilibrium. In this movie, a dictatorship makes use of drugs that suppress the emotions of people as a means of controlling the population.
- V For Vendetta. In an all-controlling, dystopian future, the subject of the government's many experiments plots his revenge upon the establishment that created him and destroyed so many others.

- X-Files: Fight The Future. Two FBI agents discover a global conspiracy that seeks to influence and control the life of everyone on the planet.

- Star Wars. An intergalactic war initiated by an ambitious politician who seeks to consolidate his power and set up a universal dictatorship.

- Nineteen Eighty-Four (1984). This film features an authoritarian society that is being governed by a Big-Brother figure as well as its elitist Inner Party. The system makes use of mind control as well as perpetual wars to maintain its hold on the citizens.

- The Matrix. Perhaps the most popular of the lot, this movie features a world beyond that of what we know and suggests that everything around us is but a mere illusion.

- The Devil's Advocate. A small town attorney is offered the chance of a lifetime but discovers later on that the price for it is more than he ever bargained for. Features Al Pacino in the role of Satan.

- Tomb Raider. The villains of this film are explicitly revealed to be members of the Illuminati order and are seeking control of a very powerful artifact. As to what exactly they would be using this artifact for, one can only guess.

The Illuminati Influence on Music:

When it comes to the music scene, the prevalence of Illuminati-related myths and even its symbols are far more obvious. In fact, it has become quite the trend for many artists to play around with the idea. Conspiracy theorists believe that not everyone in the scene is truly associated with the order, but there are a great number of them who are involved. However, contrary to the general opinion about pop stars and musicians being inducted into the order, they say that these people merely act as pawns for the Illuminati and are not really a part of it.

Much like governments and multi-national companies, conspiracy theorists say that the Illuminati has also infiltrated the highest ranks when it comes to the entertainment industry. These are the people who call the shots and can just as easily give and take any artist's fame. Think of it as signing your soul over to the devil in exchange for success in the industry. All you really need to do is perform according to the order's wishes and spread their propaganda to an even wider audience.

There are many popular artists who are said to have made this deal; among them, Jay-Z and Beyonce are the biggest names. They often make use of Illuminati symbols during performances as well, with Jay-Z taking the pyramid as a trademark hand gesture for his label. Illuminati and New World Order imagery are quite rampant in many music videos as well as song lyrics. It may seem like harmless poetry at first, but a closer inspection and a bit more understanding of the Illuminati agenda will allow a person to see with more clarity.

Chapter 4: Illuminati Symbolism, Rituals and Occultism

There are many different symbols that are associated with the Illuminati and the orders rituals. Many of these symbols can actually be seen on a daily basis, going past unnoticed until you've opened your mind to their other possible meanings.

Here are a few of the most familiar ones:

- All-seeing eye on top of a pyramid. This combination is one of the most popular symbols for the Illuminati. The eye is a representation of the Illuminati rule while the pyramid symbolizes the hierarchy of power, in that there are very few at the top and a great number at the bottom.

- Reversed pentagram. Known to many as a symbol of evil, it represents the god of the underworld's attack on heaven with his horns pointed upwards.

- All-seeing eye. This represents the Illuminati's ability to see everything and be in control of it. It is also said that it shows how they are capable of being everywhere, having infiltrated many different places to plant the seeds of their master plan.

- Owls. An owl is the representative of wisdom for many different cultures. In Illuminati symbolism, however, it represents the order's enlightened state of mind. They see themselves as the wisest and therefore, they must govern the planet. The symbol of Minerva has also been used by the Bohemian Grove elite as well as by the Minervals within the Bavarian Illuminati.

- Obelisks. Obelisks are used to mark the Illuminati's different centers of power. In Washington D.C, it has been used to show their military dominance. The ones in New York and London are said to represent their financial superiority.

How are these symbols used?

Just observe how many celebrities have taken to using the "one eye" symbol and turning it into a trend that people have completely lapped up. The image of having one eye exposed and the other covered is representative of the all-seeing eye. Celebrities like Lady Gaga, Kim Kardashian and Rihanna have all used this imagery numerous times, making it a well-known pose for many people to copy.

Another popular hand gesture would be the *"Okay"* sign that also forms the number six. Without the Illuminati context, this hand gesture is often used to indicate that "Everything's fine" or "I'm okay." However, for the members of the Illuminati it is meant to symbolize the Triple 6 or the number of the beast. In other words, it is also a pledge of allegiance to Satan.

Besides these, there are also different types of secret handshakes that members of the order use as a form of greeting each other. However, more often than not, these handshakes are for the exclusive use of higher ranking members and not for everyone who is a part of the order to know.

The Illuminati and Its Rituals:

One might think that such a seemingly modern and focused order would have no use for archaic rituals. This is most certainly not the case when it comes to the Illuminati, conspiracy theorists say. In fact, their rituals are no different from the ones conducted centuries ago - starting with animal sacrifices. For what reason? The Illuminati are firm believers in the spiritual realm; and in connecting with it through these rituals, they seek to control the powers behind all of it. For these people, more power keeps them in business for longer.

Conspiracy theorists believe that there are six different branches of learning within the Illuminati. Sciences and spiritual are two of the most important, but are also the most unique to each other. It has also been said that regardless of which department a member came from, they are required to go through spiritual rituals during high days. This is an important aspect of their being part of the order itself.

The Celtic branch of the spiritual believe that there is power being passed during that moment between life and death. This is the focal point of one ritual wherein adults and children are tied down whilst an animal is bled on top of them. In doing this, it is their belief that the person would receive power from the departing soul of the animal.

Note that these are all information forwarded by conspiracy theorists and much like many other theories associated with the Illuminati, they have never been concretely proven.

Chapter 5:
The Illuminati and Freemasonry Connection

When it comes to speaking of powerful secret societies, there's another order whose name is almost synonymous with the Illuminati despite claims that they are entirely different entities.

The Freemasons are basically a fraternal organization, older than the original Bavarian Illuminati. Their origins can be traced to the local fraternities that were formed by the stonemasons as a way of regulating a mason's qualifications as well as their interactions with both authorities and clients. The comparison with the Illuminati stems from the fact that the two share a number of similarities and have crossed paths more than once.

There may be a connection between the Freemasons and the Illuminati but the bond itself can be difficult to document. It is general knowledge that there was an Illuminati representative during a Freemason convention in 1782. This happened in Wilhelmsbad, Hesse, Germany, and was sanctioned and under the protection of the Duke of Brunswick. However, it must also be noted that Freemasons are a much older order and that they have been around since the 16th century and share the same practice of enlightened values with the Illuminati. They believe in the equality of all men as well as the existence of a Supreme Being. The Freemasons constantly practice charity as well. Certain practices may differ from one lodge to another, but the loyalty of its members are sealed by an oath, a promise to the brotherhood.

Another similarity between the two orders would be the fact that they're both magnets for controversy, persecution, and criticism. There are conspiracy theorists who also suspect the

Freemasons of seeking world domination and that together with the Illuminati, they call the shots and run the world from behind the scenes. The masons also make use of the all-seeing eye as one of their symbols.

The connection between both orders was once revealed by a British author named John Robinson. He wrote a book in 1798, one that detailed all the connections between different groups and the brewing conspiracy against all the governments and religions in Europe. His book, along with that of Abbot Agustin Barruel, placed all of the blame upon Adam Weishaupt for his involvement in the Bavarian Illuminati and the spread of the Enlightenment ideology. Both book authors were royalists and argued that the French Revolution was the work of different groups - Freemasons and Illuminati included. The authors put forth the theory that they influenced the minds of the content peasants and converted them from Religion to Atheism, from being decent to being dissolute, and from utmost loyalty to deadly rebellion.

But are these claims false? Not quite. The notion that secret groups influenced and contributed to the spirit of the French Revolution is one that is not entirely unfounded. Consider the fact that the more rationalist Freemasons, along with the Illuminati, certainly posed a significant threat to the European oligarchies of that time - all of whom depended upon the power of the Roman Catholic Church to provide legitimation. There are plenty of historians who agree, many secret societies made it their purpose to spread anti-monarchist ideals and opposed the church openly. For these secret societies, the church was a hindrance to progress, scientific development, and actual freedom. However, to say that they were the primary cause of the revolution itself has not been proven.

The Primary Difference Between the Two Orders:

If we're to take the Illuminati and compare them with the Freemasons, the most glaring difference between the two would be their overall goals as an order. The Illuminati, as suggested by various conspiracy theorists, are after the establishment of a New World Order that would completely change the way that the world functions. On the other hand, the Freemasons are seeking to create a new form of society wherein honor and chivalry are given a much higher value. They do not seek any form of dominance over the masses and instead, simply want change for the better.

Chapter 6: Popular Conspiracy Theories About The Illuminati

Over the years, countless conspiracy theories about the Illuminati, ranging from the plausible to the outright bizarre, came about. On this list, we'll go through some of the most popular ones that many people believe to be real.

- The 9/11 Tragedy

Considered to be one of the most horrific terrorist attacks on American soil, many conspiracy theorists believe it to be the work of the Illuminati in order to trigger another world war. Coincidentally, this incident became the defining moment for the US Government when it came to waging war against terrorism.

- John F. Kennedy's Assassination

It has been many years since it happened, but there is still a lot of debate and talk about the assassination of JFK. Some say that they believe the reports provided by the government, whilst others say that there are many inconsistencies in these reports that were never truly clarified. There are some people who believe that JFK was killed because he was trying to expose the Illuminati's influence on the government. He was the pawn that refused to follow orders and as such, he needed to be eliminated.

- Celebrity Pawns

The power and influence of today's big celebrities cannot be denied. They can make you buy things or even buy into an idea. Conspiracy theorists believe that some of these celebrities are actually working as pawns for the Illuminati. They're spreading the propaganda through subtle and not so subtle means. With the new generation completely glued to their every movement and trying to emulate it, this is certainly one of the best ways to get the message out there and the Illuminati is taking full advantage. Just consider all the celebrities showcasing Illuminati symbolism in their actions, performances, music videos and even song lyrics.

- Dumbing Down The Masses

It's no secret that the average individual knows more about a celebrity's life than what's actually going on around them. Well, conspiracy theorists suggest that this is also part of the Illuminati's master plan - a tactic that would distract people's attention so that no one will be able to notice their movements. It has been said that the Illuminati control the media that spread celebrity news, manipulating them to obsessively report even the smallest news about a particular personality. In the midst of all the useless information, the general public becomes continuously unaware of what's actually important.

- Celebrity Murders

Most people would chalk celebrity deaths up to something sad but not out of the ordinary. However, there are certain deaths that may have been the work of the Illuminati or so the conspiracy theorists say. This involves celebrities that may have discovered something that they shouldn't have and want to reveal it. Some celebrities may have refused to participate in the plans of the Illuminati and because they were of no use to the order, eventually eliminated. People like Princess Diana to Amy Winehouse may have died by the hand of the Illuminati, but the crime itself was conveniently covered up.

- Mind Control Programs

This would be among the scarier conspiracy theories when it comes to the Illuminati. It involves the use of mind control and programming to get people to follow their orders without question or hesitation. Imagine people who no longer have control over their own thoughts and actions being used for various propaganda purposes. Some conspiracy theorists have said that there are celebrities who may have undergone this kind of programming and that the changes are visible in the way their careers skyrocketed at a rapid pace.

Aside from the celebrities, some suggest that there are also politicians out there who have been given this type of programming; that they are merely serving as the front for the Illuminati agenda.

Conclusion

Thank you again for downloading this book!

I hope this book was able to help you learn more about the Illuminati!

The next step is to put this information to use, and begin staying cautious and wary of the things that may be being controlled by the Illuminati!

Finally, if you enjoyed this book, please take the time to share your thoughts and post a review on Amazon. It'd be greatly appreciated!

Thank you and good luck!

CPSIA information can be obtained
at www.ICGtesting.com
Printed in the USA
LVHW081100180621
690579LV00010B/277